The Ultimate Guide to Hiking, Camping, and Backpacking

TIM D. WASHINGTON

Table of Contents

Introduction

Are you planning to participate in a hiking, camping, and backpacking activity? Is it your first time? It can be challenging when you are just starting. Many newbies do not fully understand what the whole adventure entails and what supplies they need to get started. That said, they eventually end up going for a hike in the wrong clothes, backpacks, and shoes.

There is a need for an in-depth understanding of what hiking, camping, and backpacking are so that you can plan your trip better and enjoy the adventure to the fullest.

So, what is the difference between hiking, camping, and backpacking? You may be thinking, "Hiking is a group of travelers with huge backpacks walking through a thick forest". Well, if this is you, I won't judge! The good thing is that you think that hiking is an entertaining activity. At least, you are aware that it involves putting your right foot forward and then overtaking it with the left foot as many times as the trail will take you.

Anyway, let's cut to the chase; hiking is all about walking long distances for fun, navigation, and health purposes. In other words, you could be bushwalking, tramping or rambling. One thing that you should keep in mind is that hiking is quite different from a normal walk. It is a little informal and usually done in the woods or mountains.

You must be thinking, 'but how do I start hiking, camping and backpacking?' Before you start these activities, you have to make sure that you are ready both physically and mentally.

This book offers you all the information you need to know before going on a hiking, camping, or backpacking adventure.

CHAPTER ONE

Hiking, Camping, and Backpacking

There are many activities that people can engage in whenever they go outdoors to explore the beauty of nature. Hiking, camping, trekking, and backpacking have become very popular for fitness and recreational purposes.

You may think that these activities are the same, but the truth is they are different from each other. The information here will help you learn the differences, and you will begin to appreciate how unique each activity is.

Hiking

Of all the outdoor activities, hiking is the most challenging but rewarding. This is mainly because it may involve going through long stretches of rough terrain before reaching the peak. Typically, hikers do follow a nature trail or path that has already been pre-determined by professional hikers. The main aim of hiking is to enjoy nature from a different viewpoint and getting a lot of fresh air.

Since this kind of activity is more challenging, short-hike participants are recommended to bring necessary gear and daypacks containing food, supplies, and other tools they might need during the adventure.

However, we have hikers who would hike for several days up to weeks. This group of hikers requires larger backpacks filled with equipment and supplies. Regardless of what kind of hiker you are, you can hike to get fit and achieve a different form of satisfaction. Most hikers integrate their hobbies when they wander, like doing photography and journaling while appreciating the beauty of nature.

Camping

Camping is one of the most popular recreational outdoor activities. Don't get this mixed up. Camping is not your average summer camp where you send off your kids during school breaks. Instead, camping is an outdoor activity that requires you to travel and stay in a place that is closer to nature.

Whether it is near a forest or lake, people would usually set up a campsite and spend a couple of nights there. It involves pitching a tent in an open space to serve as your shelter and a place where you can keep your important belongings for the entire duration of your stay.

Others may choose to go camping by the lakeside cabin. This ensures that they have access to all the amenities they might need, such as potable water and power. Some people would use their vehicles for camping, such as campers, caravans, or motor vans.

The most exciting thing about camping is that people set up a camp on terrains as well. These may be out in the wild (Maasai Mara-Africa), open territories, and publicly owned land. It is common to confuse camping with backpacking, but the truth is that these two are quite different from each other. For instance, in camping, you stay overnight in a tent at a campsite, but you may or may not set up a camp overnight when backpacking.

Backpacking

Backpacking is one of the outdoor recreational activities that entail prolonged journeys with a backpack. In other words, all the equipment that you might need is in your backpack, including food, water, sleeping bags, clothes, and other supplies.

When you engage in this kind of outdoor activity, you will need to walk several miles for a day up to weeks carrying your backpack. On the other hand, campers can leave their stuff at the campsite, car, or van.

Backpackers would usually stay outside under the stars in their sleeping bags or a tent during nighttime. However, this may not always be the case for others who prefer to spend a night in a cheap hotel or hostel nearby.

Considering that backpackers bring everything they need throughout their journey, their bodies cannot carry too much heavy stuff. This is the reason why they need to plan their trip well and choose only the essentials.

Factors to Consider When Planning a Hike, Camping, and Backpacking

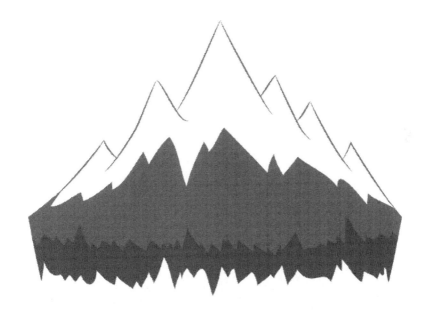

As the saying goes, "Fail to plan, and you plan to fail," preparation and planning are everything as far as camping, hiking, and backpacking are concerned. There are several factors that you have to consider for the success of every outdoor activity. Some of these factors include:

Where to go

Before you can even start preparing for anything else, you have to know the exact location. You cannot plan well if you have no idea where you are going. So, when planning for recreational outdoor activities, you have to know your route, campsite, and the nearby landmarks.

Having this information goes a long way in helping you to navigate well. If you are a beginner, you must choose a not too complicated or too challenging hiking or backpacking place. This ensures that you will be able to manage the challenges and enjoy the adventure.

Route

Knowing your route is an important thing to consider when going on a trip outdoors, especially if you are a newbie. When choosing for a place, make sure to look for flat, short-distance trails that do not have as much elevation. As you go along and accomplished several trips, you will be able to determine your physical capabilities and limitations if you have plans of going on a more challenging route.

It would be best to select a route that stays close to civilization, so you can get help if anything untoward happens. Well, I don't mean that you should not enjoy the wilderness. But for a beginner, you should choose a route that is not too far from roads and small towns.

Selecting a campsite

For your early camping adventures, you must go to a more established campsite. Besides the fact that they are easy to find, there is a high chance that they have facilities that can make the whole experience less tedious.

For example, you can have bear-proof food storage or bear poles. Therefore, if you are a beginner, you can save yourself from learning how to hack the food back trick. This is because the established campsites are most likely to have many people coming in, which adds safety whenever you need help.

Get as much information as you can about the campsite beforehand. Most of the information that you need is available online or on the site's local guidebook. If you are going to a campsite with dirt floors, it is easy for you to pitch a tent. However, if you are staying in a campsite with wooden flooring, pitching can be a little tricky. Therefore, before you go, plan things accordingly and bring all the necessary equipment with you.

One more thing you should consider when going on an outdoor trip is looking out for a freshwater source. Water is essential for survival and you will also need it for cleaning and cooking purposes. In more established campsites, you will have access to pre-built facilities like a potable water source and a fire pit.

For most people, the favorite part of camping, backpacking, and hiking is sitting around a bonfire at the end of the day. You can share stories while cooking some marshmallows. Some would even level it up and create their own version of S'mores. There is always something magical about the outdoor experience. That is why many people consider it as one of the best recreational activities.

Find out more about the local setting

Did you know that conditions can change even though they are a short distance apart? Therefore, it is important that you conduct comprehensive research of the local surroundings you are planning to visit. Some of the things that will help you are to check whether they have wildlife, fires, and litter. The truth is, different areas often have certain dangers like lions or bears, hence the need for you to have all the necessary precautions in place.

The other thing is the weather condition of that particular place. Knowing about the weather in the area you plan to visit goes a long way. This will help you plan and pack what you will need to avoid situations that might end up in disasters. If you are smoking, you must be careful in disposing of lit cigars that might cause forest fires by accident.

Who to go with

Indeed, planning for your first hiking, camping and backpacking can be super-exciting. You will find yourself getting carried away in most cases, and you end up bringing the whole family and inviting some friends too!

In as much as this might sound fun at first, this can be intense for some people. If you have a physically less-abled member of the family, try to be careful with them. It would be best not to bring small kids and the elderly along when planning to go on a more challenging activity like hiking or backpacking. The main reason for this is that their bodies may not be fit enough to tolerate the long walks, especially when going through rugged terrains.

Starting with outdoor recreational activities requires you to learn how to take care of yourself first. Once you have mastered a few tricks here and there from a couple of trips, you can now tag your children along for day hikes. Provided that the area is family and kid-friendly.

The same applies to pets. If it's your first hike to a new place, it would be better not to bring your pet. There are a lot of things that you need to put into consideration when bringing pets, especially if they are small. They may end up getting tired fast, and you will need to carry them everywhere. They may also cause problems when dealing with some wild animals. Either way, you do not want to put yourself in such situations when you are just a beginner.

What equipment you will need

Part of the preparation is ensuring that you have all the right equipment for the trip. I recently went on a backpacking trip to Australia. Trust me, it is not fun if you do not have the right equipment. I rented a flimsy tent that had missing pieces. It was crazy being out there with a half-broken tent! Therefore, you must invest in high-quality gear that you can rely on no matter what conditions you could get in.

You would also need survival skills when going out for an intense trip. You have to make sure that you are physically and mentally ready for whatever challenges you might encounter along the way.

Basic navigation skills

When people think of navigating through the woods or any place for that matter, the first thing that comes to mind is a GPS. Well, this is a good idea, only until it starts failing! The truth is, when preparing to go hiking, camping, and backpacking, some of the things that you will need for proper navigation is a good old-fashioned compass and map. Trust me; you will need it because it is extremely important to know the right way from where you are coming from to the place you are going to.

Physical readiness

Do you have any health conditions? Are you currently taking some medication? Before planning on a trip, it would be better to check with your practitioner first if you are fit for the kind of activity you want to partake. You have to make sure that you can manage any physically strenuous activities.

Hiking and backpacking involve walking on a long terrain for hours for a couple of days or up to weeks. Such activities can be overwhelming, especially if you are not physically fit. It becomes even more challenging since you will be carrying a huge and heavy backpack everywhere you go. Therefore, your body must be on tiptop condition to overcome all the challenges that might come your way when going on an adventure.

The best way to train is to go on more leisure types of outdoor activity like camping with short-distance trekking. You could spend a day or two in the woods or near a lake to learn and practice basic survival skills. Once you have gained enough experience and skills, you can then move to a more challenging type of activity.

Test your equipment

Remember when I said that I went on a backpacking trip to Australia with a flimsy tent? Yes, this happened mainly because we failed to test the tent before heading out. When you are out in the middle of the woods, the last thing you'd want is to have a tent with missing parts or any equipment that is not functional.

It would be better to check all your gear and equipment days before your trip to prevent such incidents from happening. This way, you will have enough time to go through each of them and assess their functionality. If needed, you can get a new one from your local store.

What is the weather like?

When planning your trip, it is highly recommended to check the weather forecast. Doing so will let you know when is the best time for you to go on an outdoor adventure. Mishaps could happen when the weather is bad, and of course, nobody wants to have that.

It would help to bring the essentials with you, like things that could protect you from extreme weather conditions because sometimes the weather can change so fast. Prepare your clothing and make sure that you have something to shield you from the rain and keep you warm during cold and windy nights. Jacket, raincoat, blanket, and boots are just some of them.

Do you have emergency plans?

Before you head out on your trip, you should provide your family members at home with your travel or route plan. This tool will show them the exact path you are about to take and keep track of your journey. In case of emergency, they can seek help, and the authorities can easily locate where you are. Calling your family from time to time during your trip is also helpful because they will know exactly where you are at a specific time. Updates are very important when you are away from home.

Indeed, planning is a very critical step. Make sure that you have the best route that it is suitable for your level of experience. Know what equipment to carry for all types of weather conditions. Test them before you leave for the trip to know if they are working well. Bring enough food and drinks to keep you energized throughout your journey. A little extra would be great too!

If you plan to go on a long outdoor trip, it would be best to have some knowledge about first aid. Learning first aid is beneficial for everyone because accidents can happen anywhere you are. You may have to deal with some minor injuries or health issues while you are out there. Getting help from someone may not be possible at times because of poor cellphone signals in the location. Hence, you have no one but yourself to attend to any medical emergency that you are in.

CHAPTER TWO

What Do You Need for a Hike, Camp or Backpacking Trip

After you have identified where you are going, the next step would be to prepare the items to bring with you during the trip. Whether you are going for the first time or as a well-experienced backpacker, it is important to have a checklist. It can be written on a piece of paper or a mini notebook like a travel planner.

You need to write down all the things you need, like food, drinks, clothing, and personal hygiene products. Have a separate checklist for your first aid kit and camping gear. This will avoid having to miss anything important when going on a trip. Don't bring more than you can carry if you plan to go hiking or backpacking. Leave the luxuries and focus only on the essentials.

It would also help to determine the trip duration, the weather, and how remote the location is. This will give you a hint of what items you need to bring how much. Listed below are the items you need to have on your checklist:

- Backpack
- Hiking boots or shoes
- Tent
- Sleeping bag and sleeping pad
- Cookware and kitchen utensils
- Stove and fuel
- Matchsticks and lighter
- Food and Water
- Water containers and water-treatment supplies
- Clothes (shirts, jackets, pants, socks, gloves, etc.)
- First Aid Kit
- Hygiene products
- Flashlight and headlamp
- GPS, personal locator, navigation map, and compass
- Sunglasses and sunscreen
- Insect repellent
- Knife and small repair kit

SUPPLIES NEEDED

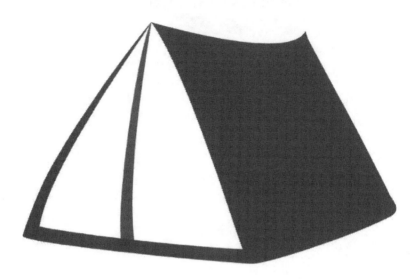

Tent

Having a tent when going camping or backpacking is essential. It is the main item on your checklist that ensures that you are protected from harmful elements during the night. It also serves as a shelter and a place where you can keep your belongings during your stay.

Most tents usually range from 2-5 pounds and are enough for at least two people. This is the most common size. However, if you are a minimalist, there are smaller ones than these. When choosing the right camping tent for you, you must look at the interior space and durability of the material used. It would be better to get one that is lightweight, spacious, and very easy to set up.

Backpack

Just like tents, having a backpack that is of good quality is critical for any outdoor adventure trip. Most backpacks range from ultra-light, which is suited for short distance hikes, to fully-featured models specifically designed for a longer backpacking trip.

Look for durable ones that have separate sections so you can organize your stuff well. Check if you feel comfortable with it, especially when you need to carry a piece of heavy equipment with you. Loosen the straps when packing and then adjust them when wearing. Your backpack must be tight enough for carrying comfortably.

The duration of your trip is the best indicator of which type of backpack you should bring. You should also consider the size of your equipment and other supplies you will need on your journey.

For a 3-day backpacking trip, you will need about 35-50L bag capacity. It is enough to carry a small tent, sleeping bag, sleeping pad, layers and extra clothing.

Sleeping bag

When hiking, camping, or backpacking, you must always carry a sleeping bag with you. It is where you will spend a good night's rest after a long and tiresome day.

If you love going outdoors, investing in a high-quality sleeping bag is recommended. It could be one of the most expensive things that you need to purchase, but the good thing is that it could last for years. Sleeping bags come in many forms, from plush mummy bags to lightweight quilts. It is important to get one that you will feel more comfortable in.

Moreover, it is recommended to choose a style and temperature rating that is suitable for your destination. You will find that car camping sleeping bags are usually cut wider, providing more space but less efficiency for holding body heat (not advisable on extra-chilly weather).

Sleeping Pad

Once you have the sleeping bag of your choice, the next most important thing is getting a sleeping pad. It ensures that you get maximum comfort since it can serve as insulation that protects you from the cold ground.

Closed-cell foam sleeping pads are your best option. Many backpackers go for a "short length" foam pad because it is lighter (if needed, you can put some extra clothing under your feet for added insulation). Winter camping: An insulated, high R-value air pad works well for cold air temperatures.

When choosing a sleeping pad, keep in mind that the higher the R-value, the more insulation you get, it works well for cold temperatures. One of the best sleeping pad models available in the market is the Therm-a-Rest, which has been at the top of the list for over a decade. The NeoAir-Lite is also popular among backpackers. Brands like the REI Flash can offer comfort and value for money as well.

Backpacking Stove

When going on an outdoor adventure, food is vital as it nourishes your body and gives you the strength to keep moving. If you are traveling for several days, there is a high chance that you might not be able to carry that much food in your backpack, along with other essentials.

There will come a time that you need to get your food from what is available around you, like fish from a lake or edible mushrooms from the forest. Hence, the need for a backpacking stove. You will find different models in your local store, from compact to a more complex kind. When choosing the best stove for your trip, consider durability and the type of fuel you will need.

If you plan to go camping, you should go for stoves that are big enough to hold large, heavy pots and pans, which is necessary in preparing meals for larger groups. MSR is a leading brand when it comes to campsite cooking, and DragonFly, is their most sought-after gourmet stove.

Other popular camping stove models include the Jetboil Flash cooking system known to boil water fast and costs only around $100. The other one is the MSR PocketRocket 2 that is compact, light, and cost-effective. Make sure that you test your stove before the trip to check if it is working well.

Food

As mentioned earlier, food is essential when engaging in an outdoor activity like hiking, camping, or backpacking. You should bring enough food to cover the entire trip and some extra. This includes items that you can have for breakfast, lunch, dinner, and snacks.

Most people would go for canned products, while others would go for dehydrated foods. Opt for the ones that could give you more nutrients as they can provide more energy. You can also find dried food products that do not require cooking and hence fewer dishes to clean.

Some instant food that does require cooking, like noodles, is quick and easy to prepare - you only need to put them in boiling water for a few minutes.

The best brand of dehydrated food is Good To-Go because they mimic real food. Other options are the Backpacker's pantry, Mountain House, and the AlpineAir, to name a few. The good thing is that these companies also make breakfast and lunch items.

Whenever going on an outdoor trip, you should bring extra food with you because some trips could take longer than you initially planned. Energy bars are a good option because you can bring many since they don't take too much space in your backpack. Furthermore, they can provide you with a quick source of energy.

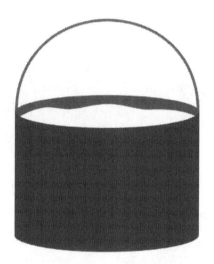

Kitchenware

When going out on a long-distance trip, kitchenware is necessary. Many people end up using an all-in-one stove system for boiling water and cooking food. You should also bring lightweight kitchen tools like a pot, plate, cup, and utensils. Avoid the heavy and expensive kind. You can find many good deals for kitchenware that you can bring on your trip.

When looking for cookware, the ones made of Titanium are likely to cost more than others because they are non-porous, do not corrode, and do not leach. In general, it is safe for cooking food and highly durable.

You can also find cookware that is made of aluminum; they are lighter but less durable. They tend to be bigger in size, soft, and dents easily. Another kind of cookware is made of stainless steel, which is affordable and durable, but the downside is that they are heavier.

Your target weight will depend on the kind of materials you choose. Opt for one that is light but durable at the same time. You can also buy them in sets so you could choose which is suitable for each trip.

Water purifiers

Water treatment options that are available today include gravity filters, UV, pump, and chemical-based purification tablets. Full-on purification is usually for high-usage areas where both human and animal waste is of great concern.

In as much as there are so many filtration options available in the market, one of the best we have come across so far is the Platypus GravityWorks 4L which is quite convenient and works fast. With this system, all you have to do is fill up the bag with water and hang it to a tree to allow gravity to do the rest of the work. If you are out hiking for only a day or two, you can choose to bring water purification tablets.

Other popular backpacking water filters and purification systems include - Steripen Ultra UV Water Purifier, Katadyn Hiker Water Filter,

Grayl GeoPress Water Purifier Bottle, MSR Guardian Purifier, and MSR Miniworks EX Water Filter.

Water bottles

The next thing that you have to prepare before your trip is having enough water supply. With this, you will need clean bottles for proper storage.

The good thing is that there is a wide variety of water bottles ranging from BPA-free plastics to stainless steel and collapsible bottles. You can get these from your local store, most of which have lightweight material and affordable options all year round.

If you are looking to have a durable water bottle, Klean Kanteen has a wide-range of backcountry-ready water bottles, cups and canisters. They are loved by many outdoor enthusiasts and nature lovers.

Other popular backpacking water bottles include - Hydro Flask Wide Mouth, CamelBak Chute Vacuum, YETI Rambler Vacuum Bottle, and GSI Outdoors MicroLite 720 Twist Vacuum Water Bottle.

Headlamp

Bringing a headlamp is one of the most important things that many people tend to forget. Trust me; if you forget it the first time, you will not repeat it the second time. When climbing a mountain or engaging in any other nighttime adventures, you must see where you are headed, hence the need for a headlamp.

Most of them are affordable, but you also need to check their durability and brightness. You should also consider the battery life so you could bring extra batteries if needed.

The best headlamp models in the market today are the Fenix HL60R and Petzl's Duo S, which has a maximum brightness of 1,100 lumens and a beam distance of 650 feet. Other popular headlamp models include - Black Diamond Spot 350, BioLite HeadLamp 330, Petzl Actik Core, Petzl Tikkina, and Princeton Tec SNAP Modular Kit.

Navigation map and compass

The oldest practice of navigating through a new route is by using a map and a compass. They are the most reliable navigation methods — but it's no good unless you know how to use them. The most commonly used by backpackers is the baseplate compass, which has a liquid-filled compass face connected to a flat, clear piece of plastic. It is very affordable and has a see-through design, which makes it easy to use with a map.

Checking your location using a compass and map is easy, but it comes with some caveats. First, you must find at least two known landmarks, like mountains and lakes. If you can find a third landmark, then that's even better. Also, keep in mind to adjust for declination.

While GPS systems are available on your watch or other handheld devices, the truth is that they are prone to failing. It would be good to have a backup plan, and bringing a map and a compass is extremely helpful, especially if visiting a place for the first time.

Additionally, there are so many smartphones today that have a hiking app on them, and they function the same way as a GPS. Ensure that you check the connectivity requirements beforehand and have enough battery to avoid disappointments during your trip.

Before going out on your trip, it would be better to familiarize yourself with the trail and landmarks nearby to keep you on the right track.

Firestarter:

When going on an outdoor adventure, you should always have reliable tools for starting and maintaining a fire. You can bring a disposable butane lighter and waterproof matches.

A firestarter is something that can help you ignite a fire. The good ones are those that can start a fire quickly and can withstand rain or wind. Other helpful supplies in creating a fire include dry tinder, candles, and wood chips soaked in resin.

FOOTWEAR AND CLOTHING

Hiking shoes and boots

Choosing the proper footwear is important when hiking or backpacking because you will spend most of your time walking. Today, the market is slowly shifting from high-end model shoes to more lightweight hiking boots and shoes primarily because they are comfortable to wear, especially for a long-distance trek.

Indeed, there are so many kinds of hiking footwear available in the market. One of the best is Salomon's X Ultra 3 Mid GTX which is durable and flexible. There is an equally good pair from X Ultra 3 GTX, a lower-cut, and a more lightweight version. Other popular hiking shoes include -   Salomon X Raise GTX, Salomon X Ultra 4 GTX, Danner Trail 2650, Keen Targhee Low Vent, Arc'teryx Aerios FL GTX, Oboz Sawtooth II Low, La Sportiva Spire GTX, and Asolo Agent Evo GV.

Hiking socks

When choosing hiking socks, look for ones with the right height and level of cushioning for your boots or shoes. Most of them are made of wool or cotton material because they add protection and comfort to your feet. The best hiking socks have the ability to keep your feet dry, regulate the temperature of your feet, and can protect your feet from blisters.

High-end hiking socks offer temperature regulation, odor resistance, and incredible moisture wicking. The popular ones are from Darn Tough Micro Crew Cushion, which is known for its premium quality products.

Hiking pants

Many people often overlook the importance of having good hiking pants. When going through a bushy trail, you need to wear something to protect your skin from getting cuts. Furthermore, it would be best if you got something that is made of breathable material so that you will feel comfortable in warm weather conditions.

Make sure that your pants are durable and stretchable enough to deal with any activity. At present, you can find pants that are made of water-resistant fabrics, zip-off legs, and articulated knees, making them suitable for intense outdoor activities. In short, you have to look for pants that have a good balance of performance and comfort.

Hiking shirt

Just as hiking pants are essential, the kind of shirt you choose is equally important. In as much as there are plenty of options available in the market, you have to choose something that can resist extreme weather conditions. Since you could only bring limited gear, choose your clothing wisely. Comfort and protection should be on top of your list. Bring shirts that you can wear when the weather is hot and something you can put on when it gets chilly.

Smartwool Merino 150 offers a wide range of lightweight shirts and even cheaper options. You can also choose to go for a short or long-sleeved shirt. The latter is best not only during cold weather conditions but also to protect your skin from the sun's scorching heat and insect bites.

Rain jacket

Even if there are no possible rains in the forecast, you must remember that the weather conditions can change fast, hence the need for waterproof gear in your backpack. You can go for rain jackets or raincoats for this purpose.

If you are hiking during the summer, you must take a lightweight rain jacket like the ones from Marmot PreCip. They are made of lightweight material that offers impeccable wind and water protection as well as breathability.

Synthetic jacket

It would be suitable for early morning walks or nighttime adventures to have a piece of clothing to keep you warm. Many people would sleep in their jackets for extra comfort and warmth.

Patagonia Down Sweater has a wide selection if you are searching for a good synthetic jacket or insulated vest. Their jackets are well-known for their extreme comfort, versatility, and durability.

Baselayers

Many hikers usually forget about baselayers, but they are very easy and compact to fit in your backpack. They could offer you extra warmth in the tent or when on the trail.

Most base layers are made from ultra-soft as well as odor-resistant merino wool. You can also find some that are made of polyester material. You must select one that is warm, soft, odor-resistant, and moisture-wicking. The Smartwool Merino 250 ¼-zip is perfect for these types of activities.

OTHER ITEMS

Trekking Poles

Trekking poles are extremely helpful, especially when going on a long-distance trek. They basically take the pressure off your feet and knees, making the hiking experience easier and more comfortable.

You can take your pick between aluminum and carbon material with foam and cork grips, as well as telescoping and folding options. Whatever your choice is, opt for the one that looks sturdy and made of high-quality materials.

Gloves

When the temperatures drop, gloves can make your trip more comfortable. They don't just make you look stylish, but they also offer you another layer of protection from the cold weather. This is especially the case if you do not intend to bring with you a hooded insulation piece. Additionally, if you are using a quilt or a full-on sleeping bag, having gloves can give you extra warmth and comfort.

Here are some of the best hiking gloves you will find in the market - Cevapro -30°F Winter Gloves Touchscreen Gloves, Black Diamond Soloist Gloves, The North Face Etip Gloves, Marmot Evolution Glove, Outdoor Research VersaLiner Glove, Extremities Antora Peak GTX, SEALSKINZ Ultra Grip Glove, Mountain Hardwear Power Stretch Stimulus Gloves, and Outdoor Research Alti Mittens.

Chair

Bringing a lightweight backpacking chair could also give you comfort during your camping trip. In as much as they are easy to carry, you can leave them at your campsite since they are not necessary on the trail. It is that one item that keeps you from sitting on the ground and keeps your butt dry. You can use them for relaxation or during mealtime.

When choosing a camping or backpacking chair, it is recommended to stay under two pounds. Getting chairs that are heavier could outweigh the benefits.

Camp footwear

After a very long, tiresome day, you probably would like to rest your feet before going through another long trail the next day. Nothing feels better than taking those hiking boots and socks off and then replacing them with fresh and breathable camp footwear.

Some of the footwear you can bring with you are Crocs and other outdoor sandals or flip-flops. Most of them are made of lightweight material and therefore wouldn't add too much weight to your backpack. Trust me; your feet will thank you for it.

Camera

Make your trip memorable and capture those wonderful moments by bringing a camera with you. You can choose to bring your compact camera or just use your smartphone camera. Either way, you will find it more rewarding because you will always have something to remind you of your adventure to that specific place.

You can even share the pictures that you took with family and friends so they too can appreciate the beautiful places that you went to. Maybe with this, you could inspire them to go with you on your next trip.

DSLR cameras are your best option if you want to do nature or night photography. Even though they are heavy and quite expensive, they take far better photos than just a regular point-and-shoot camera. Another option is a mirrorless camera, like the Sony A7R III, which has become a favorite among many travelers.

Sunglasses

Fashion-wise, many people are wearing sunglasses because it adds style and glamour. But in terms of backpacking or hiking, sunglasses are beneficial for you because they can protect your eyes from the sun's harmful UV rays. Moreover, they can shield your eyes from dirt when the weather gets windy.

You can choose your sunglasses from a wide range of brands like Oakley, Native, and Smith. If you have a budget, you could get the polarized glasses that do a pretty good job at reducing the glare when on water and snow.

CHAPTER THREE

Practical Tips for Your Adventure

Go with an experienced camper, backpacker, or hiker

When you are a beginner at hiking or backpacking, it would be beneficial to bring someone with you who's had an experience so he can guide you.

As a newbie, you may not be confident about your ability to navigate through the woods. And having someone to walk you through the whole process could help keep you away from harm. They could give you tips on how to pack your things before your trip, choose which gear to bring, pitch a tent, and go through a very challenging trail.

Do an overnighter for a start

When it comes to starting your first backpacking trip, it would be good to keep things simple. In other words, before you can go for a long-distance and more strenuous backpacking or camping trip, you should start with an overnighter that you can easily manage.

The main reason for this is that most long-distance trails require more logistics and physical exertion since you will be walking for long hours. It would be good to try for one night to learn the basics and enjoy the experience. This way, you will know what to expect on your succeeding outdoor adventures and prepare for them.

Only travel a modest distance

As said earlier, it is better to try shorter distances when starting. Many beginners may get super excited about going on a long-distance trip without really considering what their bodies can cover comfortably. Know that not everyone can carry a huge backpack for several days. This is the reason why you should give yourself time to prepare for a more challenging trip.

Hiking for hours is no easy task, especially if your body is not used to it. You have to carry your weight and also your backpack, which could be very tiresome. So, to avoid too much exhaustion, foot sores, and muscle cramps, travel just 5 miles or less. This way, you will learn to hike at a much comfortable pace.

Select the most convenient hiking routes possible

Did you know that loop hikes and out-and-back routes are quite easier to plan? It is also recommended for a beginner because the start and the end are on the same trailhead.

However, if you plan a point-to-point trip, there is a high chance that you have to place cars at both ends of the route, which could be very expensive and complicated to plan.

Do some homework on your gear

Preparing for your gear ahead of time is the right thing to do. It would be best to research different brands for the specific equipment you plan to bring on your trip and start comparing their special features and prices. Look for the ones that are made of high-quality materials and cost-efficient.

Create a checklist for all the things you need to buy and where you intend to get them. At present, people are no longer limited to buying in local stores because, thanks to technology, we can now purchase the products from different online stores and have them delivered to your doorstep. But, before you purchase anything, always have an idea of what options are available to you so that you can make the right choices for your trip.

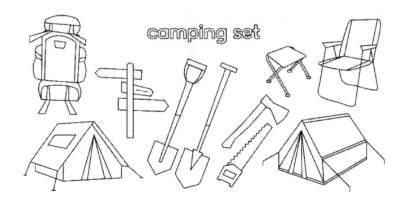

Rent some gear to save on money

Outdoor activities such as hiking, camping, and backpacking require high-quality gear, which can get very expensive! If you do not have a budget to purchase everything you need for your first trip, you can borrow from a friend or rent.

If you are traveling with someone more experienced, there is a good chance that they know someone you can borrow your gear from. Additionally, you can get some items for rent from an outdoor specialty store or similar online services.

You can rent things like sleeping bags, backpacks, stoves, tents, and other backpacking necessities. As you continue to gain more experience from your travels, you will also learn more about the best brands for specific gear. Choose the ones worth investing in, especially if you have plans of making it a regular activity.

Invest in high-quality footwear

There is nothing that can ruin your trip and cut it short much faster than shoes or boots that do not fit well or that fall apart. Therefore, if you want to have a beautiful and comfortable experience out on the trail, better get high-quality footwear.

If you plan on trekking in the rain or crossing lots of water streams in cold weather, you must consider getting yourself waterproof boots. However, if you plan on hiking in warm-humid weather, wearing waterproof footwear will trap in lots of moisture and warm air, which could cause blisters.

On the other hand, if you carry a load of 25 pounds backpack or less, it is better if you choose a low-cut shoe for your hike and travels. However, if your backpack is more than 25 pounds, you will need a full boot to give you the rigidity and midsole structure that you will need to bear with the load on your back.

Also, you must wear them several days before your trip to check whether they fit well and you are comfortable in them before hitting the actual trail.

Layer up wisely

When out on a trip, you must choose clothes that can help regulate your body temperature in such a way that you are not too hot or too cold. If you are going on a trip during warm weather, you can pack short-sleeved shirts made of cotton fabrics. If traveling during spring, fall, or winter, make sure that you are covered in layers.

You can begin with a thin top and bottom base made of wool or synthetic fabrics. Then, the next layer would be a light or mid-weight top and bottom work over the base layer. You can also add an insulated or waterproof jacket and pants for even colder conditions. Lastly, pack some gloves and headgear to keep you from the cold.

Keep the campfire menu quite simple

In the backcountry, food tastes better when it is freshly cooked over a fire. But, you will likely arrive at the campsite exhausted and not in the mood to cook a complicated meal. Therefore, to make things simple but nourishing.

You should bring easy to prepare meal items with you that you can have for breakfast, lunch, and dinner. You can find many options, including freeze-dried and instant meals that would only require boiling water to cook.

Additionally, you can get several packets of vegetable soup along with some cans of tuna, chicken, or salmon from your local store. Stay away from food that may require lots of preparation and cooking since you can only bring limited cookware with you.

Be ready when nature calls

You have to understand that you do need to make some adjustments when out on the trail. You have to make do of what is available to you, like the woods or bushes, as your restroom when you need to ease yourself. At first, this can be discomfiting, but you'll get used to it, and the process is quite simple; ease yourself and bury your waste. Just make sure that you carry a toilet kit containing some toilet paper, wipes, and hand sanitizer.

You must also have a trowel for digging a cat hole. This may not be the most pleasant part of your adventure, but soon enough, you will start seeing it as second nature.

CHAPTER FOUR

How Do You Get In Shape for a Hike, Camp, or Backpacking Trip?

Physical fitness is a very important factor to consider before doing any strenuous activity. When you are going on an outdoor adventure, you will need to have strength and balance. You have to be physically fit to keep going for hours without getting tired easily.

Since most of the trails are rough and some even have elevations, you will need balance and strength to hold yourself up and avoid any injury. Moreover, different weather conditions could make your trip more physically challenging, like the trails could become very slippery. So, your body must be prepared to endure varying situations.

It would be helpful if you could plan your trip way ahead so that you will have enough time to get fit by having some cardio and strength exercises regularly.

Listed below are some tips to attain fitness and stay in shape before your trip:

Begin with the Basics

One of the most common kinds of injuries when out on a trail include ankles rolling and spraining. If you have a sedentary lifestyle and not that physically fit, you must start with the basic exercises. You can do some stretching first, then arm, leg, and head rotations to warm you up. Slowly do some cardio workouts like skipping rope, stationary bike, or jogging for a few minutes. Then, you can move to some exercise that will help strengthen your muscles like planks, push-ups, squats, and crunches, to name a few.

If you live near the beach, you could also include walking and running on the sand as part of your training. This workout will help build your leg muscles to protect your knees and ankles when you hit the trail.

Gradually, increase the time you spend on your workout by doing more repetitions and adding other exercises to your routine. Going to the gym is not a requirement. You can do your workout at home, in the park or beach.

Train for a Day Hike

The first thing you should try is to go out for a walk or run at least three times a week. It would be better to use the same shoes you will wear during your excursion because you can have blisters during your trip if you wore shoes that you haven't used. You can also carry a backpack with some stuff to let you get the hang of it.

If you are a beginner or haven't done any hiking for a while, you can start by going out on a day hike. This way, you'll have an idea of what you have to prepare for before going on a long-distance hike. It will also give your body time to prepare for a more arduous trip.

Best Exercises That Will Get You in Shape

Lunges

A resistance type of exercise, which is good in strengthening your lower body, quadriceps, and hamstrings. In a standing position, step one foot forward until your knee is bent and the foot lay flat on the ground. While, the other leg is positioned at the back. Do this exercise on both legs alternately.

Band Walks

Begin by tying a resistance band around your legs. Make sure that the band is just above the knees in such a way that you feel tension when you stand with legs at your hip-width. Next, stand straight with your abs tucked. Then place your hands on your hips and begin walking sideways. While you do this, you must maintain the tension of the band between your shins.

Poor Man's Leg Curl

Here, you begin by lying on the floor and then scoot the hips to move towards a little raised bench. Then lift your right leg as far as you can go while pressing the left foot into the bench. Then, clench your glutes and hamstrings while raising the hips off the ground. Repeat this on each side at least ten times.

CHAPTER FIVE

How Can You Avoid Injury While On a Steep Trail?

We often think that going to the peak of the trail is the most difficult part. The truth is that coming downhill can be tough as well because you need to create balance on your body to avoid injury. You will feel more pressure on your legs, especially on the knee part. This is because the body is holding its weight back, including the huge backpack, to resist falling.

Additionally, when you go through rocky formations, you may feel a strain on your joints. The best way to prevent this from happening is to have enough exercise or training before the hike to develop flexibility and strength.

Avoiding the Hiker's Knee

Having regular exercise can make your calves, quadriceps, and hamstrings stronger. Brisk walking or riding a bike can help strengthen your muscles and build endurance.

You can also use ankle weights. If it's your first time, use a 5-pound only, and then gradually increase the weight. When working out your hamstrings, stand and lift one of the weighted legs behind you until you achieve a right angle. Then hold it there for a couple of minutes before you lower the foot down and do the same with the other leg.

Using Trekking Poles

When walking through sloppy and steep trails, the biggest concern is the knees and the ankles. To avoid causing yourself an injury, you can consider using a pair of trekking poles.

The good thing about using trekking poles is that they help you keep your balance while on rocky terrain. They are the ones that give you that extra pair of limbs that will hold you up while navigating that rough terrain. If you have joint issues, it is even wiser to invest in a pair.

The best way to use them is to keep your arms in a neutral position. Slightly bend your elbows and then use the shoulders to push you forward. Now, use the straps to get a much more relaxed grip on the poles.

As you hike down the hill, you must keep the poles in front of you just a little. This will help shorten the strides so that the pressure on the knees is reduced significantly. However, if the trail is too steep or muddy, you can try ramming the poles into the ground and then try making sidesteps towards the poles. On the other hand, while hiking up the hill, you can use the poles to push off and not pull yourself.

Using the Right Hiking Footwear

We cannot stress this point enough! The type of footwear that you choose is very important to avoid injuries during your trip. It doesn't only protect your feet, but it should also help keep your balance. It should be comfortable and sturdy enough to support your ankles and knees.

Therefore, when you shop for hiking footwear, they must complement your fitness and packing style. While you may spend less effort in trail running shoes, you must consider getting a pair of mid-cut boots when you have a previous injury in your ankles.

Conclusion

Getting ready for hiking, camping, or a backpacking trip can be a little daunting. However, the good thing is that if you do your homework well and invest lots of your time in preparation, you could just be looking at an opportunity for endless trips and a life full of incredible adventures.

If your trip will last for several days to weeks, the last thing you would want is to get up on the third day with sores all over your body. There is no backing out when in the middle of the trail. You need to get going until the end of the trip. Therefore, you must give yourself at least a month to prepare before the trip.

Depending on how long you plan the trip, make sure that you are well prepared physically and mentally. Go out for walks and short hikes at least twice a week for a month or two. It would be good to practice a healthy lifestyle by eating nutritious food and drinking plenty of water, especially during training. Having enough sleep and rest is also vital as it will help your body achieve optimal health and well-being.

There are tremendous rewards that come along with proper planning and effort. This is because as you hit the trail and get deep into the woods. You will have the opportunity to discover beautiful sceneries, natural splendor, and solitude that many other people out there do not get the chance of experiencing.

During the night, you'll get a chance to look at the twinkling stars, far away from all forms of distractions and civilization. You start enjoying the serenity that is the uniqueness of the place, far away from the world you are accustomed to.

Good luck and enjoy!!

Made in the USA
Las Vegas, NV
29 December 2023

83688764R00037